MERRILL READING SKILLTEXT® SERIES

Going F

MW01519261

Editorial Review Board

Story Pictures

SRA/McGraw-Hill
A Division of The McGraw·Hill Companies

Send all inquiries to:
SRA/McGraw-Hill
8787 Orion Place
Columbus, OH 43240-4027

ISBN 0-02-687869-0

3 4 5 6 7 8 POH 05 04 03 02 01

SRA/McGraw-Hill
Columbus, Ohio

Which picture is different?

Directions: In each row, put an **X** on the object that is a color different from the others.

Home Practice: Point to an object in each row. Ask the child to name an object in the room that is the same color.

Which picture is different?

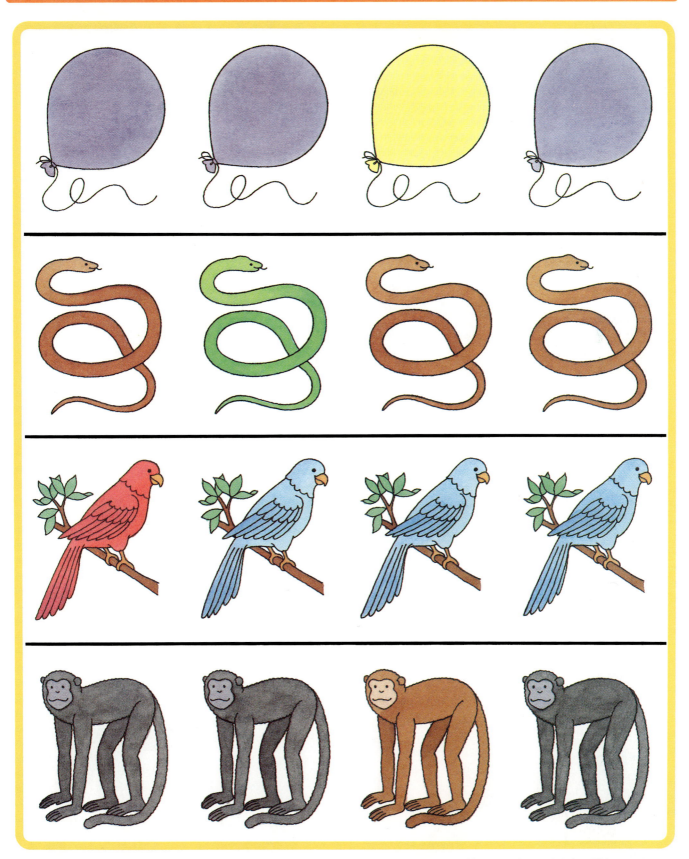

Directions: In each row, put an **X** on the object that is a different color from the others.

Home Practice: Point to an object in each row. Ask the child to name an object in the room that is the same color.

3

Find the Colors

Directions: Circle each object with the crayon that matches the color of the object.

Home Practice: Point to the pictures in left-to-right order and ask the child to name each object and its color.

Find the Colors

Directions: Circle each object with the crayon that matches the color of the object.

Home Practice: Point to the pictures in left-to-right order and ask the child to name each object and its color.

5

Which shapes look alike?

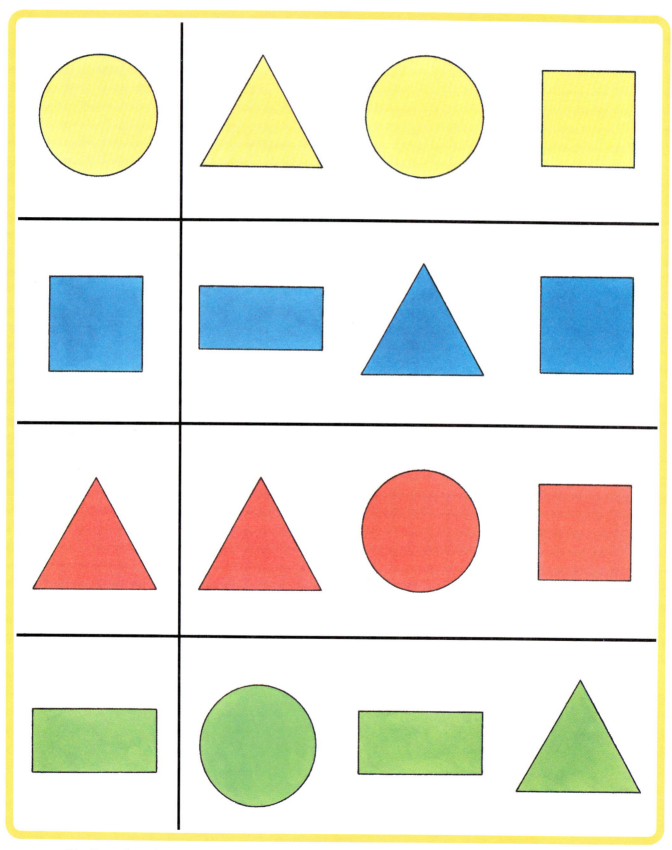

Directions: In each row, circle the shape that matches the first shape in that row.

Home Practice: Describe a shape on this page. Then have the child point to that shape.

Match the Shapes

Directions: Draw a line to connect the shapes that match each other.

Home Practice: Point to shapes at random and have the child name the color.

7

Find the Shapes

Directions: In each row, circle the shape you are told to circle.

Home Practice: Play a game by having the child point to a shape when you have described it. *(green square)*

Find the Shapes

Directions: In each row, circle the shape that you are told to circle.

Home Practice: Play a game by pointing to shapes. Have the child name each one.

9

Finish the Shapes

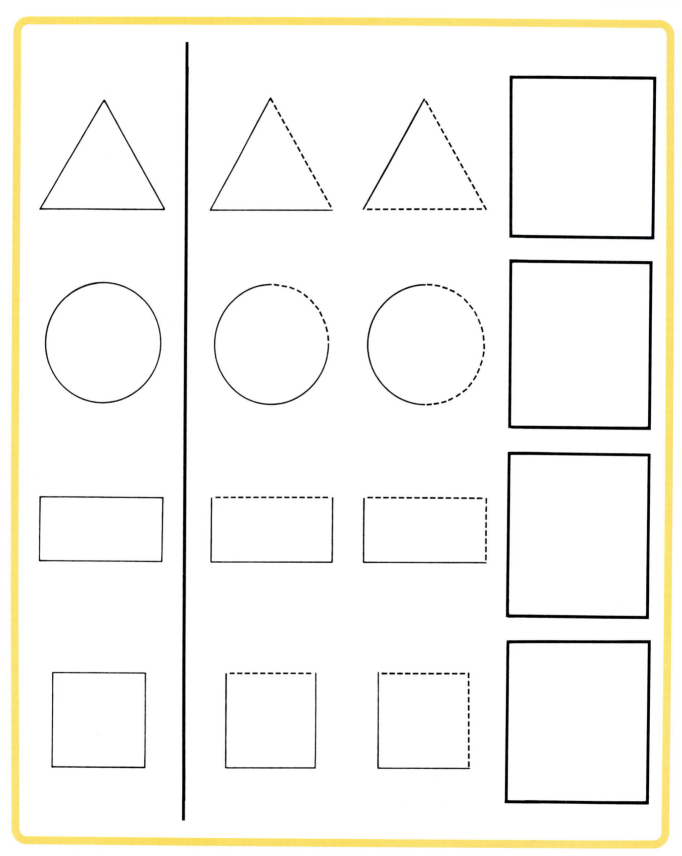

Directions: In each row, trace the dashed lines to complete the shapes. Then draw the same shape in the last box.

Home Practice: Play a game of review by pointing to a shape and having the child identify it.

How many are there?

1 1

2 2

3 3

4 4

5 5

Directions: Trace each numeral and write it. Then draw a line from the numeral to the set it represents.

Home Practice: Ask the child to name the objects. Then have the child count each set of objects.

11

How many are there?

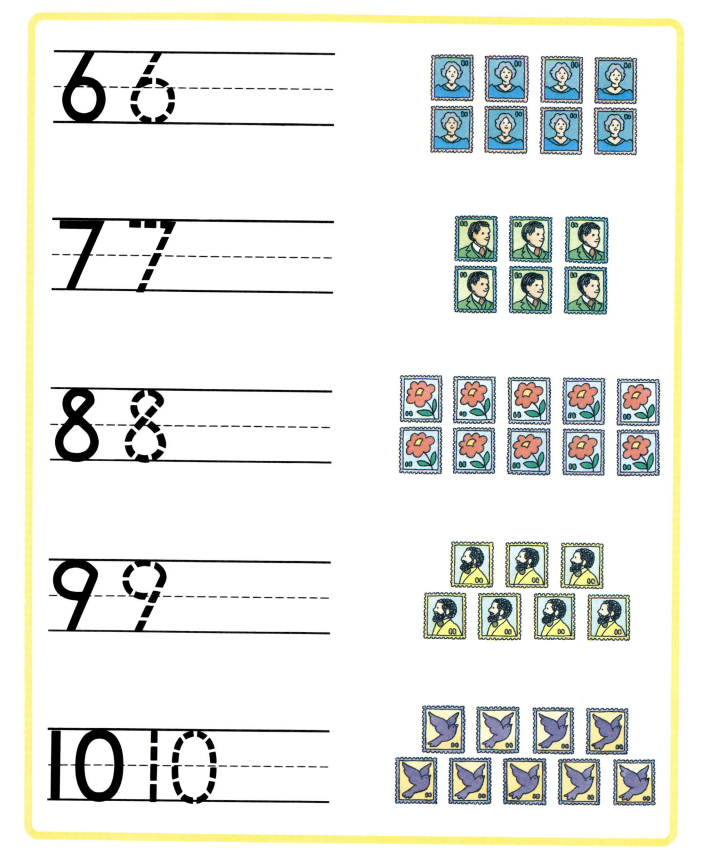

Directions: Trace each numeral and write it. Then draw a line from the numeral to the set it represents.

Home Practice: Ask the child to name the objects and tell what colors they are. Then have the child count each set of objects.

Shopping for Food

Directions: Discuss the picture.

Home Practice: Ask the child to look at the picture and describe what each person is doing.

13

What is the right order?

Directions: In the box, put a **1** under the picture that happened first, **2** under the picture that happened next, and **3** under the picture that happened last.

Home Practice: Have the child tell in correct sequence the story that is represented by each set of pictures.

Match the Letters

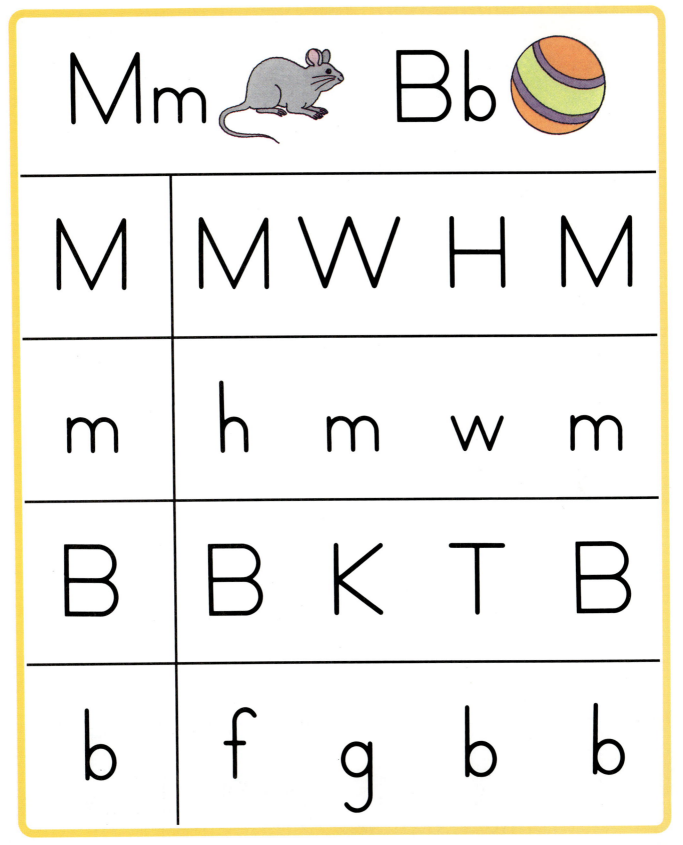

Mm	Bb
M	M W H M
m	h m w m
B	B K T B
b	f g b b

Directions: In each row, circle the letters that match the first letter in the row.

Home Practice: Point to a circled letter in each row. Ask the child to find and point to that letter in a magazine or newspaper.

15

Match the Sounds

Directions: Name the pictures. Circle each picture whose name begins with the sound you hear at the beginning of *mouse*. Then do the same thing for *ball*.

Home Practice: Ask the child to name two circled pictures from each part of the page and then find objects in the room whose names begin with the same sound.

The Sounds of M and B

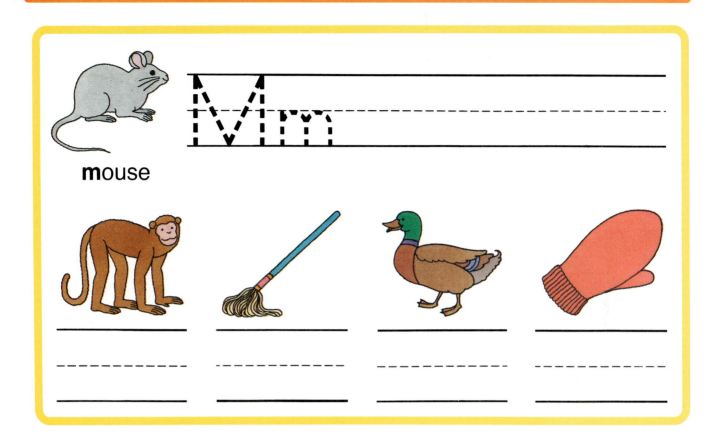

mouse

ball

Directions: Trace the letters and write them. Circle each picture whose name begins with **m** and write **m** on the line below it. Put an **X** on the pictures whose names do not begin with the sound of **m.** Then do the same for **b.**

Home Practice: Play a guessing game using the pictures. Make up clues such as this: *My name begins with the sound of m. I keep a hand warm. What am I? (mitten)*

17

At the Zoo

Directions: Discuss the picture.

Home Practice: Have the child name each animal and tell something special about it.

Match the Letters

N	P

N	V	N	N	M

n	n	m	u	n

P	B	P	P	R

p	p	q	p	j

Directions: In each row, circle the letters that match the first letter in the row.

Home Practice: Point to a circled letter in each row. Ask the child to find and point to that letter in a magazine or newspaper.

19

Match the Sounds

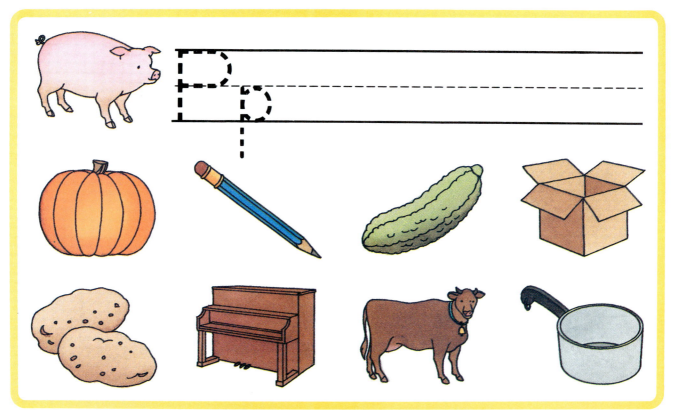

Directions: Name the pictures. Circle each picture whose name begins with the sound you hear at the beginning of *nest.* Then do the same thing for *pig.*

Home Practice: Ask the child to name two circled pictures from each part of the page and then find objects in the room whose names begin with the same sound.

The Sounds of N and P

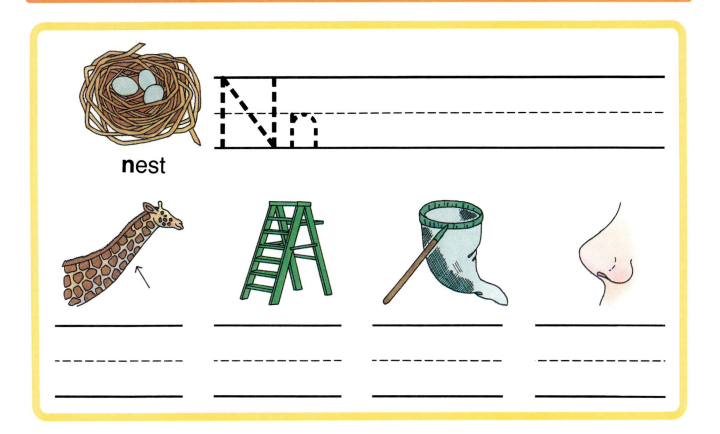

nest

pig

Directions: Trace the letters and write them. Circle each picture whose name begins with **n** and write **n** on the line below it. Put an **X** on the pictures whose names do not begin with **n.** Then do the same for **p.**

Home Practice: Play a guessing game using the pictures. Make up clues such as this: *My name begins with the sound of **n.** You smell with me. What am I? (nose)*

21

The Sounds of M, B, N, and P

Directions: Look at the letter at the beginning of each row. Circle each picture whose name begins with the sound of that letter.

Home Practice: Have the child point to and name all the animals on this page *(monkey, bird)* and all the things you wear *(boot, bow)*. Then have the child say the letter that stands for the beginning sound of each name.

On a Farm

Directions: Discuss the pictures.

Home Practice: Ask the child to identify the activity of each person in the pictures.

Match the Letters

A a 🐜	S s ☀️

A	A V A H A
a	a o a e
S	S Z G S
s	z s e s

Directions: In each row, circle the letters that match the first letter in the row.

Home Practice: Point to a circled letter in each row. Ask the child to find and point to that letter in a magazine or newspaper.

Match the Sounds

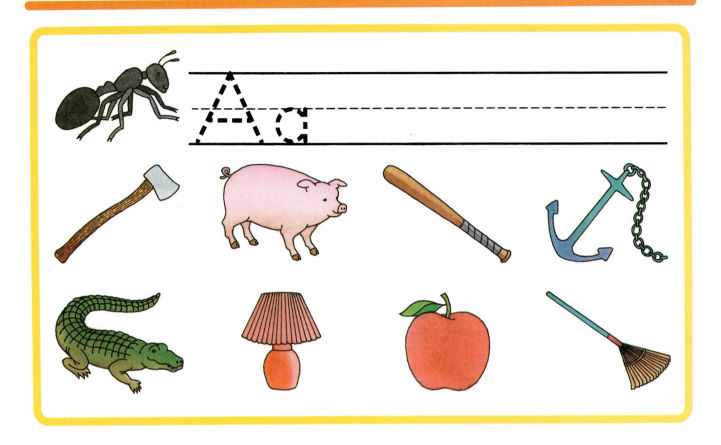

A a

S s

Directions: Name the pictures. Circle each picture whose name begins with the sound you hear at the beginning of *ant*. Then do the same thing for *sun*.

Home Practice: Ask the child to name two circled pictures from each part of the page and then find objects in the room whose names begin with the same sound.

The Sounds of A and S

ant

sun

Directions: Trace the letters and write them. Circle each picture whose name begins with **a** and write **a** on the line below it. Put an **X** on the pictures whose names do not begin with **a.** Then do the same for **s.**

Home Practice: Play a guessing game using the pictures. Make up clues such as this: *My name begins with the sound of s. You cut wood with me. What am I? (saw)*

Match the Sound

hand

a

Directions: Name the pictures. Circle each picture whose name has the sound you hear in the middle of *hand*.

Home Practice: Ask the child to point to and name three circled pictures. Then say each of these words and have the child tell you whether it has the same middle sound as hand: *sad, hot, like, tan.*

27

Which belong together?

Directions: In each row, circle the three objects that belong together.

Home Practice: Have the child name the pictures in each row that are circled and then have him or her tell how the objects are alike.

Through the Year

Directions: Discuss the pictures.

Home Practice: Have the child compare the children's clothing and the appearance of the outdoors in these pictures.

29

Which belong together?

Directions: Draw a line from each object in the first row to an object that goes with it in the next row. Do the same thing for the third and fourth rows.

Home Practice: Have the child tell you how the objects that go together are related.

Match the Letters

K k	T t

K	K	N	R	K
k	k	l	k	t
T	T	L	T	Y
t	h	t	t	l

Directions: In each row, circle the letters that match the first letter in the row.

Home Practice: Point to a circled letter in each row. Ask the child to find and point to that letter in a magazine or newspaper.

31

Match the Sounds

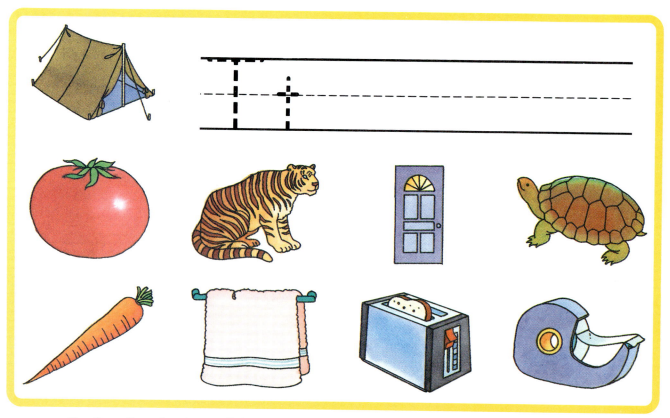

Directions: Name the pictures. Circle each picture whose name begins with the sound you hear at the beginning of *kite*. Then do the same thing for *tent*.

Home Practice: Ask the child to name two circled pictures from each part of the page and then find objects in the room whose names begin with the same sound.

The Sounds of K and T

kite

tent

Directions: Trace the letters and write them. Circle each picture whose name begins with **k** and write **k** on the line below it. Put an **X** on the pictures whose names do not begin with **k.** Then do the same for **t.**

Home Practice: Play a guessing game using the pictures. Make up clues such as this: *My name begins with the sound of **k**. I can open a door. What am I? (key)*

The Sounds of A, S, K, and T

Directions: Look at the letter at the beginning of each row. Circle each picture whose name begins with the sound of that letter.

Home Practice: Have the child point to and name all the animals on this page. *(alligator, seal, turkey, turtle)* Then have the child say the letter that stands for the beginning sound of each animal name.

Making Music

Directions: Discuss the picture.

Home Practice: Ask the child to look at the picture and describe what each person is doing.

What is the right order?

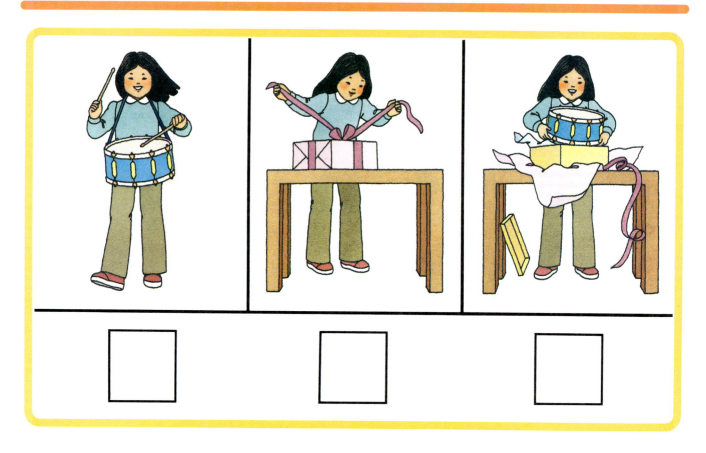

Directions: In the box, put a **1** under the picture that happened first, **2** under the picture that happened next, and **3** under the picture that happened last.

Home Practice: Have the child tell in correct sequence the story that is represented by each set of pictures.

Match the Letters

C	C	G	C	O
c	o	c	n	c
E	E	F	B	E
e	a	e	v	e

Directions: In each row, circle the letters that match the first letter in the row.

Home Practice: Point to a circled letter in each row. Ask the child to find and point to that letter in a magazine or newspaper.

37

Match the Sounds

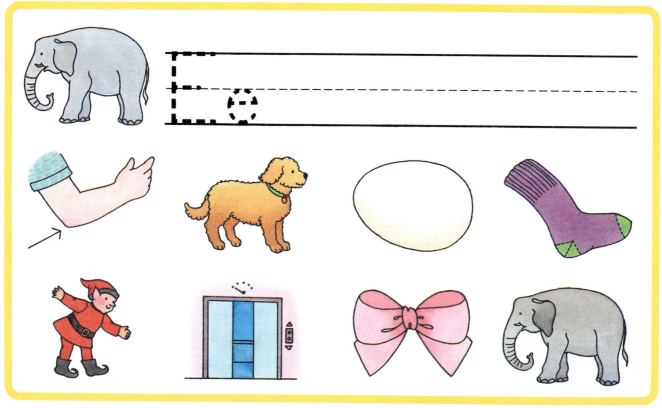

Directions: Name the pictures. Circle each picture whose name begins with the sound you hear at the beginning of *car*. Then do the same thing for *elephant*.

Home Practice: Ask the child to name two circled pictures from each part of the page and then find objects in the room whose names begin with the same sound.

The Sounds of C and E

car

elephant

Directions: Trace the letters and write them. Circle each picture whose name begins with **c** and write **c** on the line below it. Put an **X** on the pictures whose names do not begin with **c.** Then do the same for **e.**

Home Practice: Play a guessing game using the pictures. Make up clues such as this: *My name begins with the sound of* **c.** *I give you milk. What am I? (cow)*

39

Match the Sound

fence

Directions: Name the pictures. Circle each picture whose name has the sound you hear in the middle of *fence*.

Home Practice: Ask the child to point to and name three circled pictures. Then say each of these words and have the child tell you whether it has the same middle sound as *fence*: *box, pen, bike, web.*

Which belong together?

Directions: In each row, circle the three objects that belong together.

Home Practice: Have the child name the pictures in each row that are circled and then have him or her tell how the objects are alike.

41

A Hospital Stay

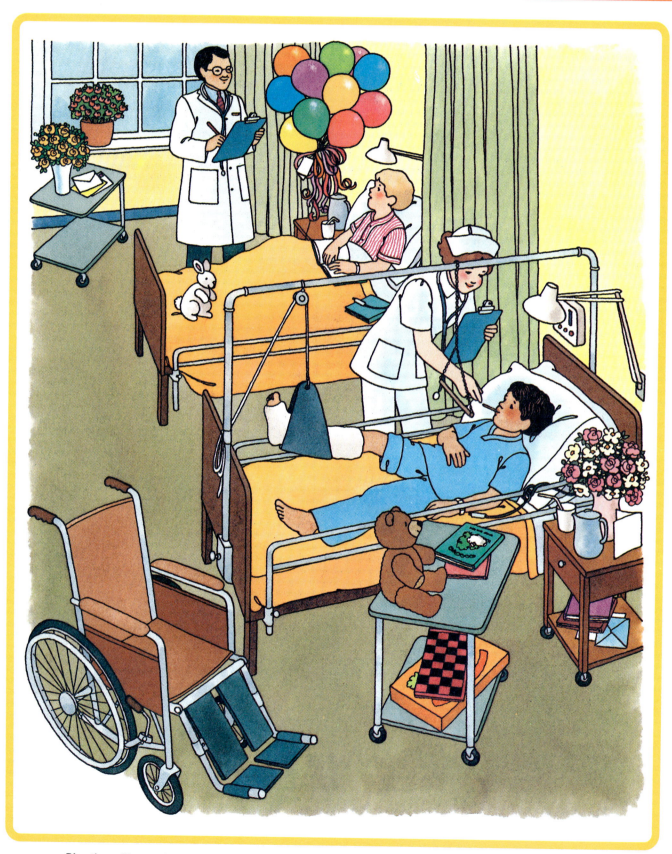

42 **Directions:** Discuss the picture.

Home Practice: Ask the child to tell what each person in this picture might be thinking or saying.

Look at the Sizes

Directions: In each row, circle the object that you are told to circle.

43

Match the Letters

F f	L l
F	T E F F
f	f l f k
L	J L I L
l	b l l d

Directions: In each row, circle the letters that match the first letter in the row.

Home Practice: Point to a circled letter in each row. Ask the child to find and point to that letter in a magazine or newspaper.

Match the Sounds

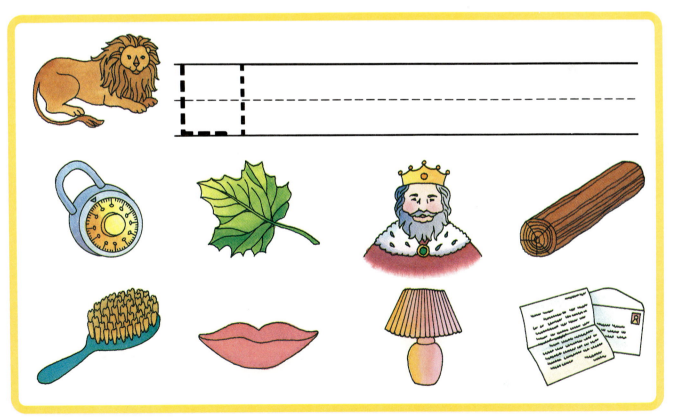

Directions: Name the pictures. Circle each picture whose name begins with the sound you hear at the beginning of *fish*. Then do the same thing for *lion*.

Home Practice: Ask the child to name two circled pictures from each part of the page and then find objects in the room whose names begin with the same sound.

45

The Sounds of F and L

fish

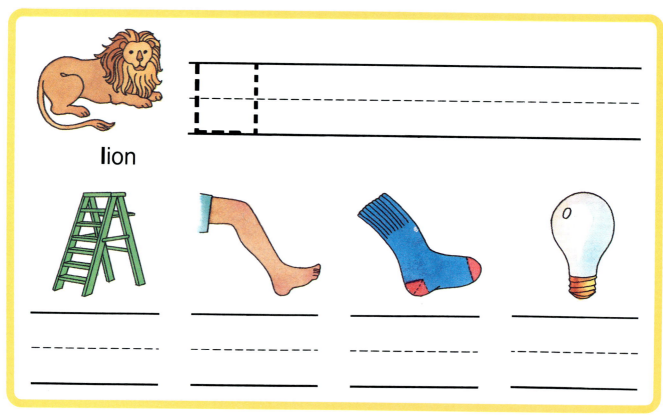

lion

Directions: Trace the letters and write them. Circle each picture whose name begins with **f** and write **f** on the line below it. Put an **X** on the pictures whose names do not begin with the sound of **f.** Then do the same for **l.**

Home Practice: Play a guessing game using the pictures. Make up clues such as this: *My name begins with the sound of l. You climb up me. What am I? (ladder)*

The Sounds of C, E, F, and L

Directions: Look at the letter at the beginning of each row. Circle each picture whose name begins with the sound of that letter.

Home Practice: Have the child point to and name all the objects that can be played (drum, piano) or with which a child can play (football, doll). Then have the child say the letter that stands for the beginning sound of each name.

47

Mailing a Letter

Directions: Discuss the pictures.

Home Practice: Ask the child to look at the pictures and describe what each person is doing.

Which belong together?

Directions: In each row, circle the picture that belongs with the first picture in the row.

Home Practice: Have the child tell you how the objects that go together are related.

49

Match the Letters

H h	R r
H	H L I H
h	d h h l
R	P R B R
r	h r r m

Directions: In each row, circle the letters that match the first letter in the row.

Home Practice: Point to a circled letter in each row. Ask the child to find and point to that letter in a magazine or newspaper.

Match the Sounds

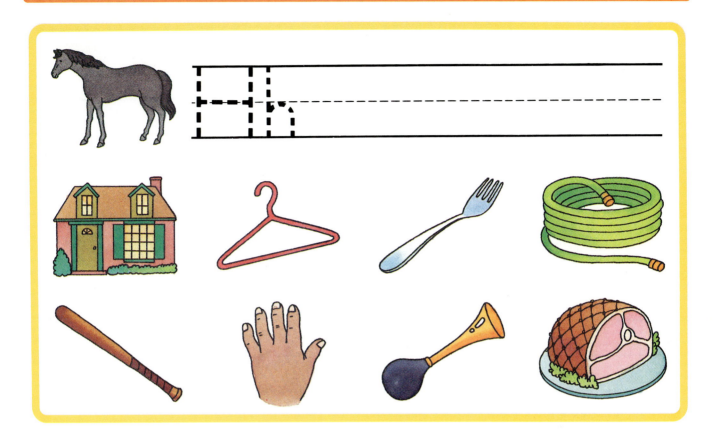

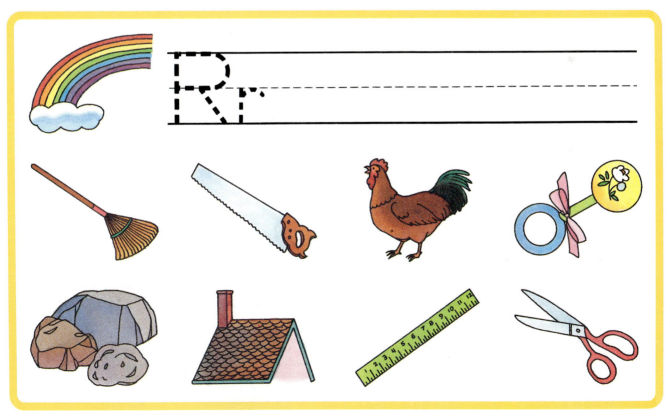

Directions: Name the pictures. Circle each picture whose name begins with the sound you hear at the beginning of *horse.* Then do the same thing for *rainbow.*

Home Practice: Ask the child to name two circled pictures from each part of the page and then find objects in the room whose names begin with the same sound.

51

The Sounds of H and R

horse

Hh

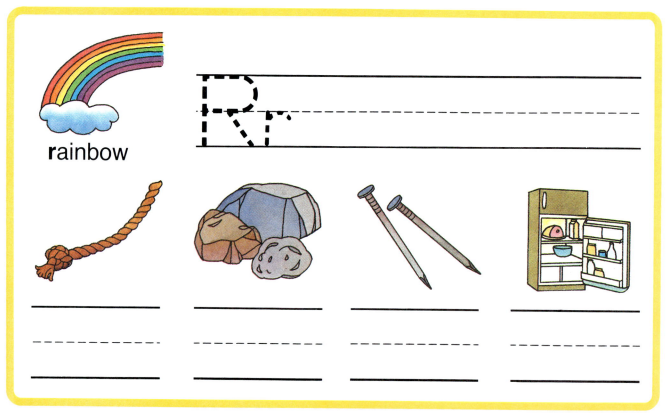

rainbow

Rr

Directions: Trace the letters and write them. Circle each picture whose name begins with **h** and write **h** on the line below it. Put an **X** on the pictures whose names do not begin with **h.** Then do the same for **r.**

Home Practice: Play a guessing game using the pictures. Make up clues such as this: *My name begins with the sound of h. You pound with me. What am I? (hammer)*

What is the right order?

Directions: In the box, put a **1** under the picture that happened first, **2** under the picture that happened next, and **3** under the picture that happened last.

Home Practice: Have the child tell in correct sequence the story that is represented by each set of pictures.

53

Dressing Up

Directions: Discuss the picture.

Home Practice: Have the child name some of the objects found in this attic. Encourage the child to tell what the boy and girl in the picture might be thinking.

Match the Ones That Rhyme

Directions: Draw a line from each object in the first row to an object that rhymes with it in the next row. Do the same with rows three and four.

Home Practice: Say a word that rhymes with one of the picture names. Have the child point to the correct picture or pictures. Use clues such as this: *Find a picture with a name that rhymes with cat. (hat, bat)*

55

Which belong together?

Directions: Circle the three pictures in each row that belong together.

Home Practice: Have the child tell you how the circled pictures in each row are related.

Match the Letters

I i	G g
I	I H T I
i	i r i t
G	C G O G
g	g y g j

Directions: In each row, circle the letters that match the first letter in the row.

Home Practice: Point to a circled letter in each row. Ask the child to find and point to that letter in a magazine or newspaper.

57

Match the Sounds

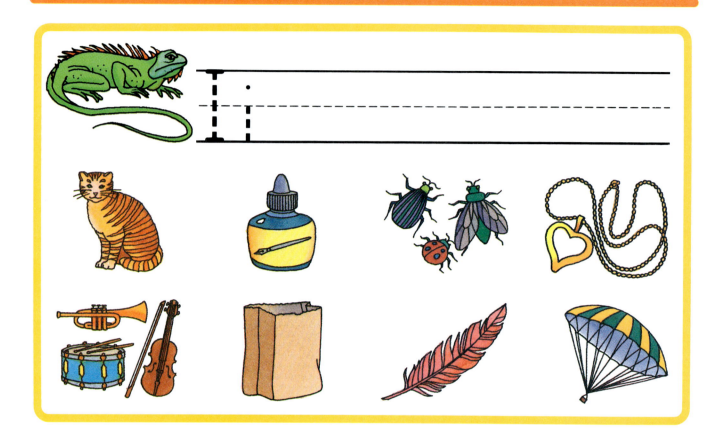

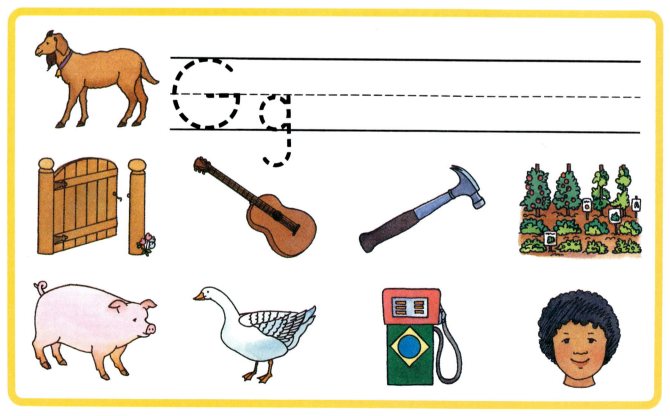

Directions: Name the pictures. Then circle each picture whose name begins with the sound you hear at the beginning of *iguana*. Then do the same thing for *goat*.

Home Practice: Ask the child to name two circled pictures from each part of the page and then find objects in the room whose names begin with the same sound.

The Sounds of I and G

iguana

goat

Directions: Trace the letters and write them. Circle each picture whose name begins with **i** and write **i** on the line below it. Put an **X** on the pictures whose names do not begin with **i**. Then do the same for **g**.

Home Practice: Play a guessing game using the pictures. Make up clues such as this: *My name begins with the sound of i. You find me in a pen. What am I? (ink)*

59

Match the Sound

chick

Directions: Name the pictures. Circle each picture whose name has the sound you hear in the middle of *chick*.

Home Practice: Ask the child to point to and name three circled pictures. Then say each of these words and have the child tell you whether it has the same middle sound as *chick*: *make, sit, sock, bib*.

The Sounds of H, R, I, and G

Directions: Look at the letter at the beginning of each row. Circle each picture whose name begins with the sound of that letter.

Home Practice: Have the child point to and name all the animals on this page. *(mouse, rooster, insects, goose)* Then have the child say the letter that stands for the beginning sound of each animal name.

61

Moving In

Directions: Discuss the picture.

Home Practice: Ask the child to look at the picture and tell what each person is doing and what he or she might be thinking.

Match the Letters

D	O	D	D	B
d	d	h	g	d
J	U	J	L	J
j	j	p	j	q

Directions: In each row, circle the letters that match the first letter in the row.

Home Practice: Point to a circled letter in each row. Ask the child to find and point to that letter in a magazine or newspaper.

63

Match the Sounds

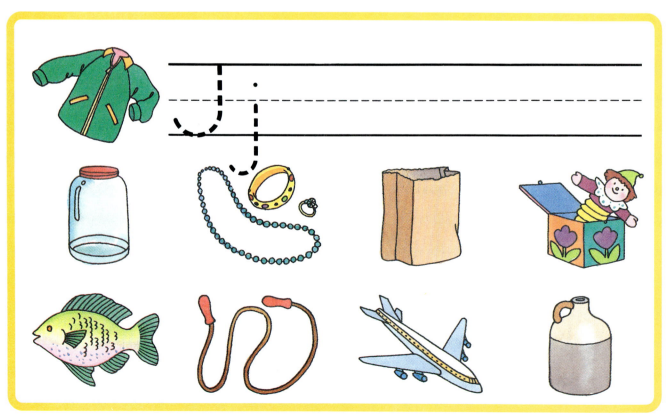

Directions: Name the pictures. Circle each picture whose name begins with the sound you hear at the beginning of *dog.* Then do the same thing for *jacket.*

Home Practice: Ask the child to name two circled pictures from each part of the page and then find objects in the room whose names begin with the same sound.

The Sounds of D and J

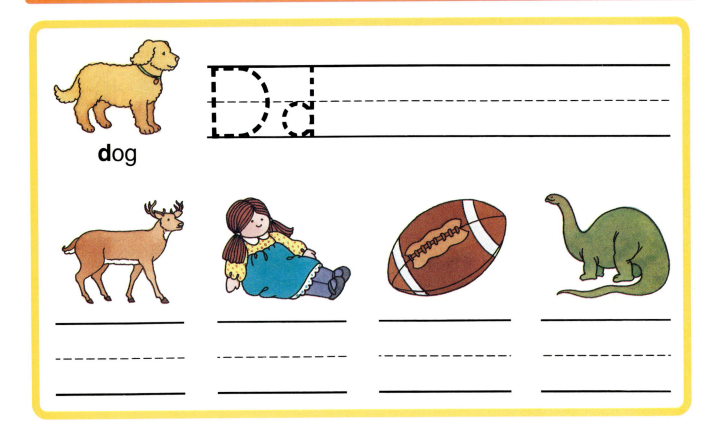

dog

jacket

Directions: Trace the letters and write them. Circle each picture whose name begins with **d** and write **d** on the line below it. Put an **X** on the pictures whose names do not begin with **d.** Then do the same for **j.**

Home Practice: Play a guessing game using the pictures. Make up clues such as this: *My name begins with the sound of j. You wear me to keep warm. What am I? (jacket)*

65

Where are they?

Directions: Circle each picture that you are told to circle.

Home Practice: Point to pictures at random and have the child describe them.

Visiting the Fire Station

Directions: Discuss the picture.

Home Practice: Ask the child to look at the picture and tell what each person might be thinking or saying.

Which ones rhyme?

Directions: In each row, circle a picture whose name rhymes with the first picture in the row.

Home Practice: Say a word that rhymes with one of the picture names. Have the child point to the correct picture or pictures. Use clues such as this: *Find a picture with a name that rhymes with cat. (hat)*

Match the Letters

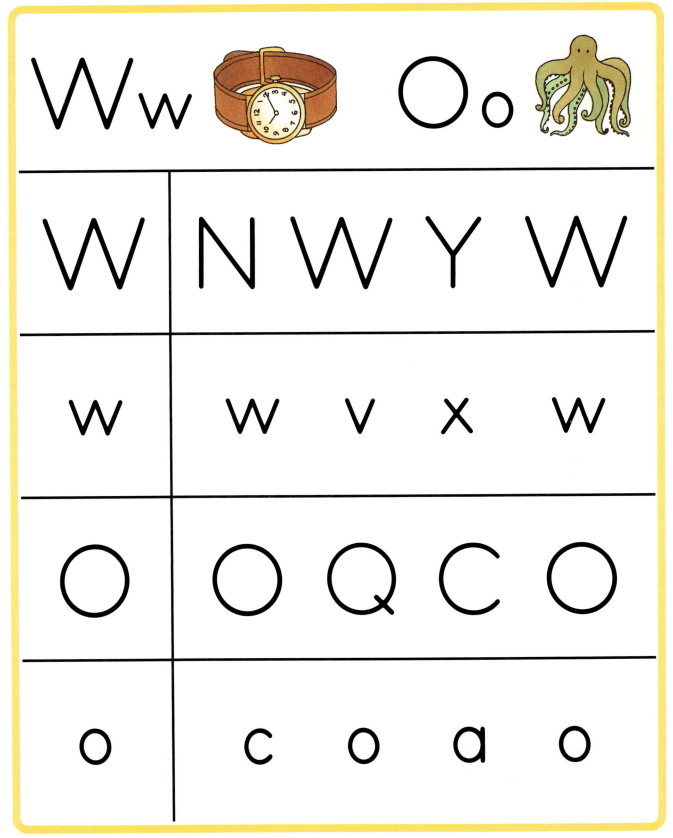

W	N	W	Y	W
w	w	v	x	w
O	O	Q	C	O
o	c	o	a	o

Directions: In each row, circle the letters that match the first letter in the row.

Home Practice: Point to a circled letter in each row. Ask the child to find and point to that letter in a magazine or newspaper.

69

Match the Sounds

Directions: Name the pictures. Then circle each picture whose name begins with the sound you hear at the beginning of *watch*. Then do the same thing for *octopus*.

Home Practice: Ask the child to name two circled pictures from each part of the page and then find objects in the room whose names begin with the same sound.

The Sounds of W and O

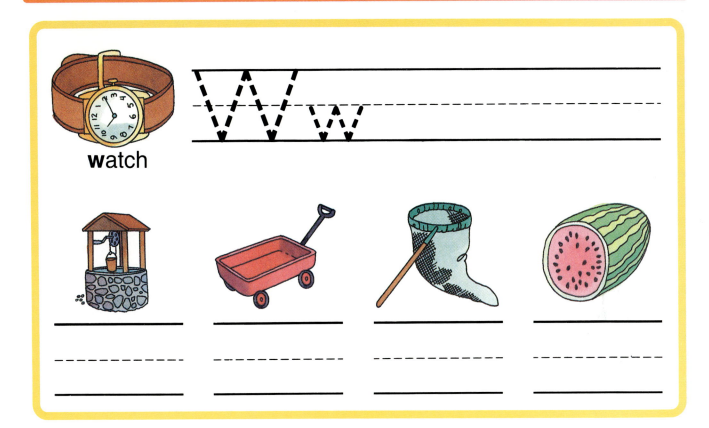

watch

octopus

Directions: Trace the letters and write them. Circle each picture whose name begins with **w** and write **w** on the line below it. Put an **X** on the pictures whose names do not begin with **w**. Then do the same for **o**.

Home Practice: Play a guessing game using the pictures. Make up clues such as this: *My name begins with the sound of w. I tell you the time. What am I? (watch)*

71

Match the Sound

mop

Directions: Name the pictures. Circle each picture whose name has the sound you hear in the middle of *mop*.

Home Practice: Ask the child to point to and name three circled pictures. Then say each of these words and have the child tell you whether it has the same middle sound as mop: *hot, red, take, box.*

The Sounds of D, J, W, and O

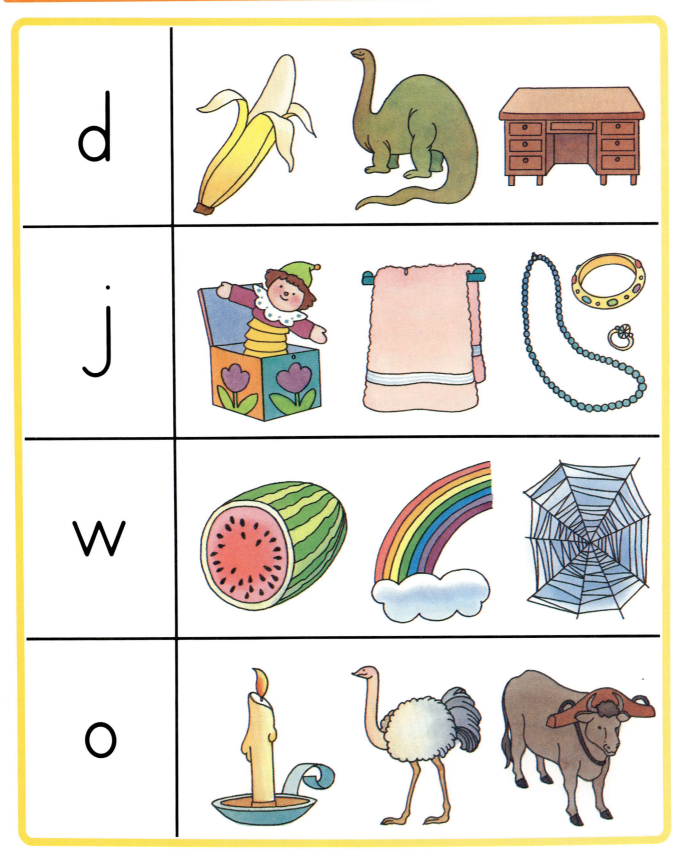

Directions: Look at the letter at the beginning of each row. Circle each picture whose name begins with the sound of that letter.

Home Practice: Have the child point to and name all the things to eat on this page (*banana, watermelon*) and all the animals (*dinosaur, ostrich, ox*). Then have the child say the letter that stands for the beginning sound of each name.

73

Making Puppets

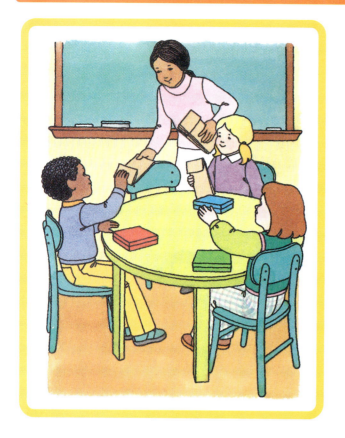

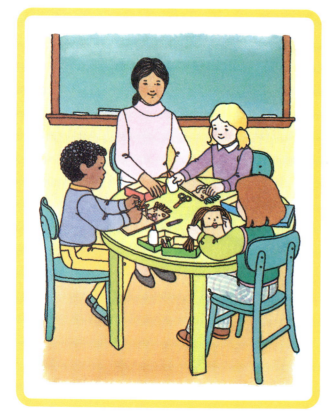

Directions: Discuss the pictures.

Home Practice: Ask the child to look at the pictures and tell what each person is doing.

74

Look at the Sizes

Directions: In each row, circle the picture that you are told to circle.

Home Practice: Point to two puppets in the same row and tell ways they are alike and ways they are different.

75

Match the Letters

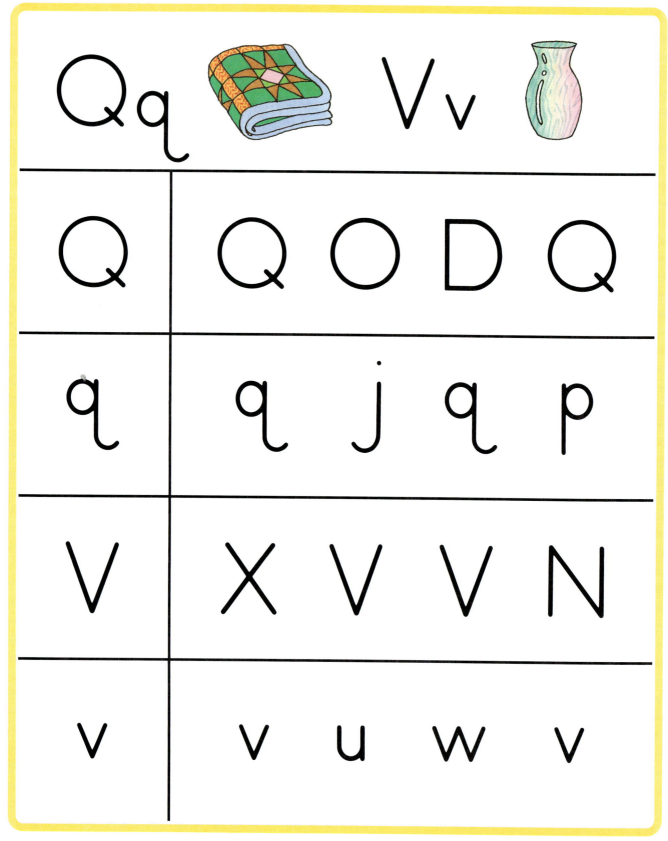

Q q   V v

Q	Q O D Q
q	q j q p
V	X V V N
v	v u w v

Directions: In each row, circle the letters that match the first letter in the row.

Home Practice: Point to a circled letter in each row. Ask the child to find and point to that letter in a magazine or newspaper.

Match the Sounds

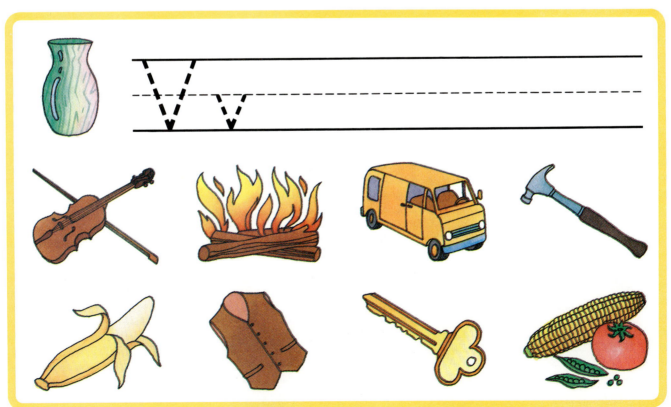

Directions: Name the pictures. Then circle each picture whose name begins with the sound you hear at the beginning of *quilt*. Then do the same thing for *vase*.

Home Practice: Ask the child to name two circled pictures from each part of the page and then find objects in the room whose names begin with the same sound.

77

The Sounds of Q and V

quilt

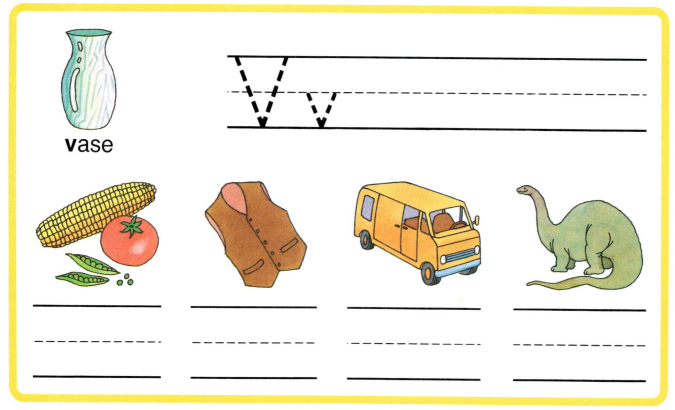

vase

Directions: Trace the letters and write them. Circle each picture whose name begins with **q** and write **q** on the line below it. Put an **X** on the pictures whose names do not begin with **q**. Then do the same for **v**.

Home Practice: Play a guessing game using the pictures. Make up clues such as this: *My name begins with the sound of q. I wear a crown on my head. Who am I? (queen)*

How will it look?

Directions: In each row, circle the picture that shows how the bag or table would look as a result of the first picture.

Home Practice: Point to a picture at random and ask the child to describe it.

79

Gym Class

Directions: Discuss the picture.

Home Practice: Ask the child to look at the picture and describe what each person is doing.

Where are they?

Directions: Circle each picture that you are told to circle.

Home Practice: Point to pictures at random and have the child describe them.

81

Match the Letters

Y y	U u

Y	Y	T	K	Y

y	v	y	w	y

U	O	U	J	U

u	u	n	c	u

Directions: In each row, circle the letters that match the first letter in the row.

Home Practice: Point to a circled letter in each row. Ask the child to find and point to that letter in a magazine or newspaper.

Match the Sounds

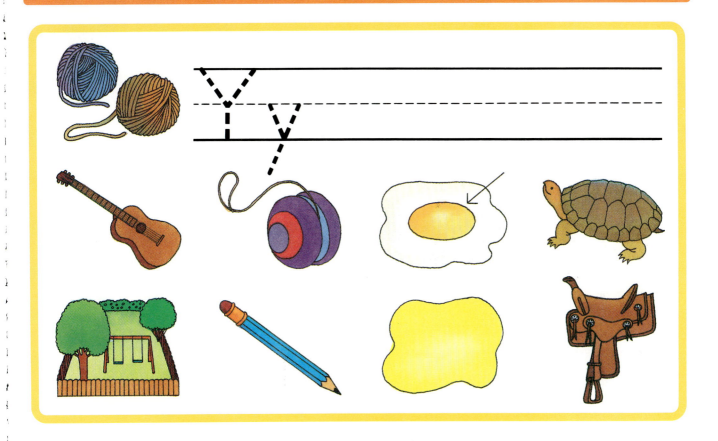

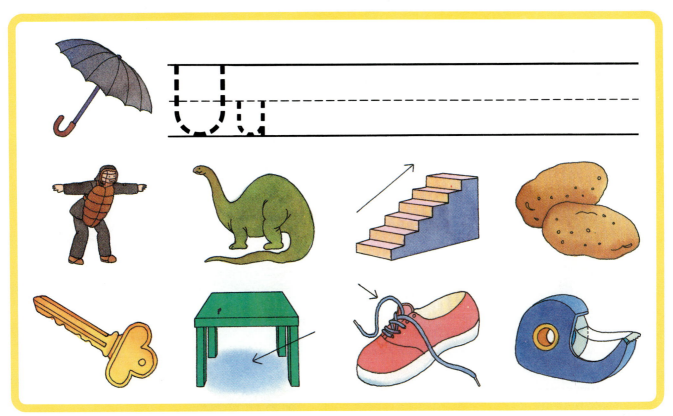

Directions: Name the pictures. Then circle each picture whose name begins with the sound you hear at the beginning of *yarn.* Then do the same thing for *umbrella.*

Home Practice: Ask the child to name two circled pictures from each part of the page and then find objects in the room whose names begin with the same sound.

83

The Sounds of Y and U

yarn

umbrella

Directions: Trace the letters and write them. Circle each picture whose name begins with **y** and write **y** on the line below it. Put an **X** on the pictures whose names do not begin with **y.** Then do the same for **u.**

Home Practice: Play a guessing game using the pictures. Make up clues such as this: *My name begins with the sound of y. You can play in me. What am I? (yard)*

Match the Sound

duck

Directions: Name the pictures. Circle each picture whose name has the sound you hear in the middle of *duck*.

Home Practice: Ask the child to point to and name three circled pictures. Then say each of these words and have the child tell you whether it has the same middle sound as *duck*: *cup, cake, bus, pet*.

A Pet Show

Directions: Discuss the picture.

Home Practice: Point to a pet at random and ask the child to name it and tell you something special about it.

Match the Letters

X x	Z z
X	Z X Y X
x	y x z x
Z	Z N S Z
z	z s w z

Directions: In each row, circle the letters that match the first letter in the row.

Home Practice: Point to a circled letter in each row. Ask the child to find and point to that letter in a magazine or newspaper.

87

The Sound of X

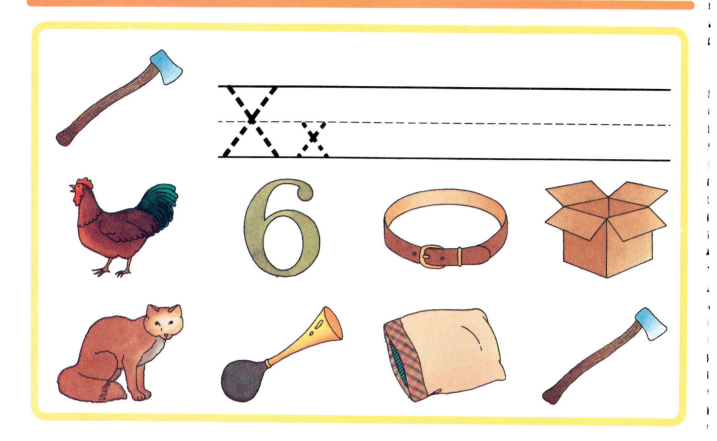

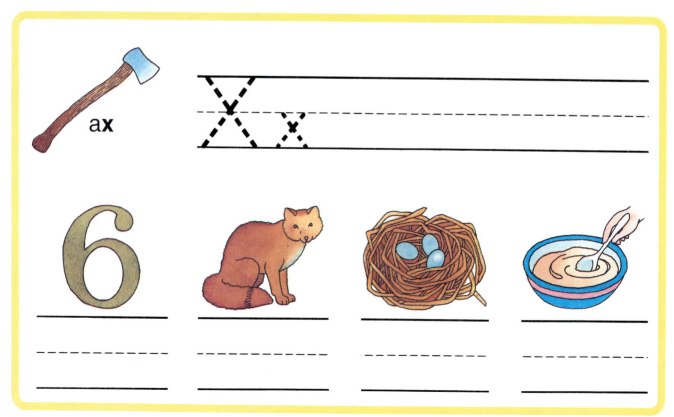

ax

Directions: *(Top)* Name the pictures. Then circle each picture whose name ends with the sound you hear at the end of *ax*. *(Bottom)* Circle each picture whose name ends with **x** and write **x** on the line below it. Trace the letters and write them.

Home Practice: Ask the child to name two circled pictures from each part of the page and then think of objects whose names end with the same sound.

The Sound of Z

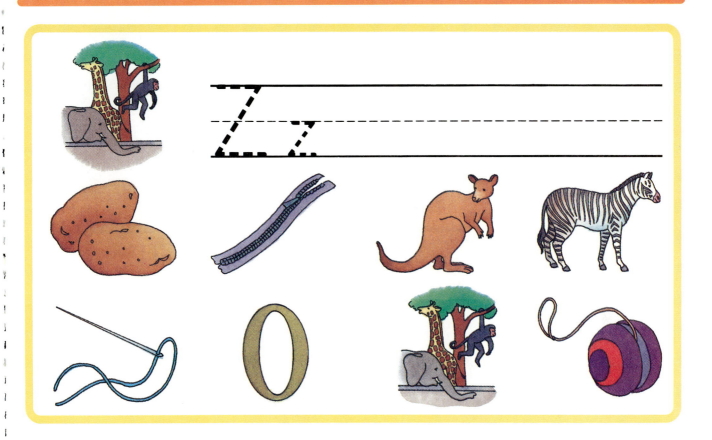

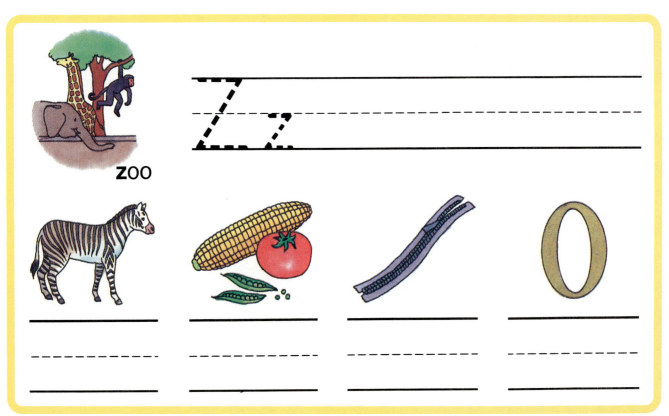

zoo

Directions: *(Top)* Name the pictures. Circle each picture whose name begins with the sound you hear at the beginning of *zoo*. *(Bottom)* Circle each picture whose name begins with **z**. Write **z** on the line below it. Trace the letters and write them.

Home Practice: Play a guessing game using the pictures. Make up clues such as this: *My name begins with the sound of **z**. I am a striped animal. What am I? (zebra)*

The Sounds of Q, V, Y, and U

Directions: Look at the letter at the beginning of each row. Circle each picture whose name begins with the sound of that letter.

Home Practice: Have the child point to and name all the things to eat *(banana, watermelon)* or wear *(dress, vest)* on this page. Then have the child say the letter that stands for the beginning sound of each name.

Which words look alike?

cat	ball	cat	cat
ball	ball	tree	ball
dog	girl	dog	dog
tree	tree	dog	tree
girl	dog	girl	girl

Directions: In each row, circle the words that match the first word.

Home Practice: Point to any two words on the page and ask the child if they match.

91

Which words look alike?

Can	Can	See	Can
you	you	cat	you
see	the	see	see
the	can	the	the
cat	see	cat	cat

Can you see the cat?

Directions: In each row, circle the words that match the first word.

Home Practice: Point to any two words on the page and ask the child if they are alike or different.

Pretest for *Going Places*

Name _____

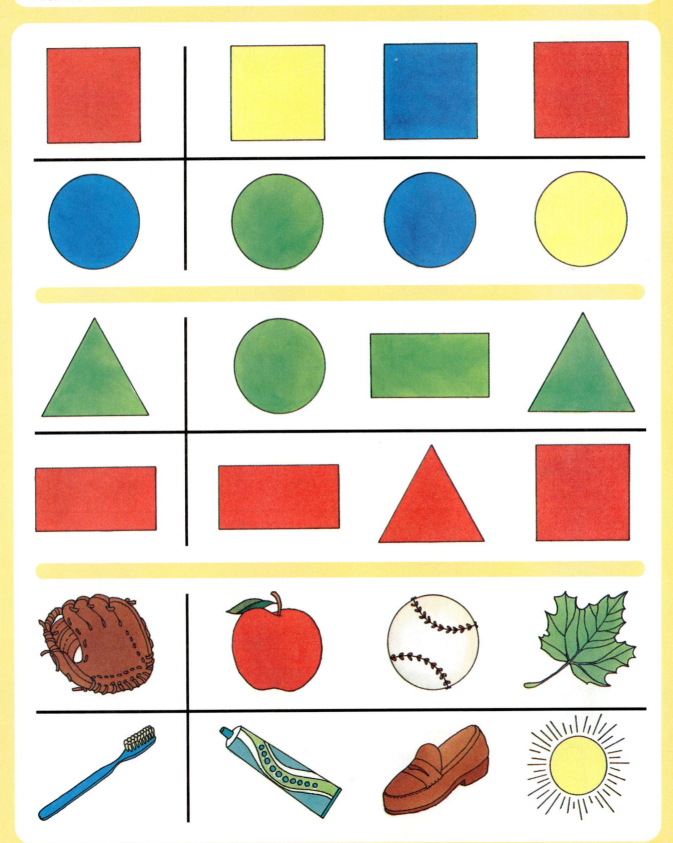

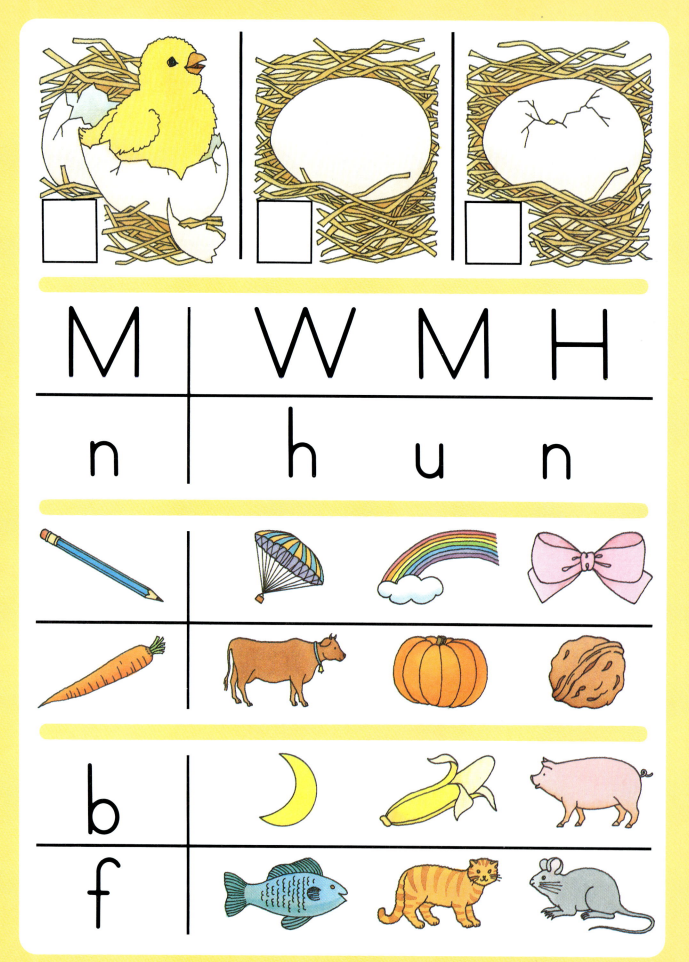

Posttest for Going Places

Name _____